Jayne Wallace is the founder and owner of Psychic Sisters, a team of 16 clairvoyants and healers working from a concession at Selfridges in London. Launched in 2006, it was the first psychic concession in a department store. Jayne has worked with a number of celebrity clients, including Kim Kardashian West, Tracey Emin and Kylie Jenner. She also writes regular columns for *Spirit & Destiny*, *Soul & Spirit* and *Fate & Fortune* magazines.

Feeling inspired?

Check out these other HarperTrue titles:

My Psychic Casebook

My **Psychic** *Casebook*

The amazing secrets of the world's most
respected department-store medium

Jayne Wallace

Harper
True *Fate*

HarperTrueFate
An imprint of HarperCollins*Publishers*
1 London Bridge Street
London SE1 9GF

www.harpertrue.com
www.harpercollins.co.uk

First published by HarperTrueFate 2015

1 3 5 7 9 10 8 6 4 2

© Jayne Wallace and Liz Dean 2015

Jayne Wallace and Liz Dean assert the moral right
to be identified as the authors of this work

A catalogue record of this book is
available from the British Library

ISBN 978-0-00-810518-1

Printed and bound in Great Britain by
RR Donnelley at Glasgow, UK

Contents

Introduction

Welcome to My Psychic World

I'm Jayne. I'm a psychic and medium, and I'd like to tell you some stories. First, I'll tell you a little about me.

I met my spirit guide when I was just five years old. A young girl came to me one night when I was almost asleep. She didn't scare me; she was very pretty and petite, with a sparkling, star-shaped gemstone in the centre of her forehead. I called her Star. Star began to tell me things that other people didn't know or talk about. I remember feeling happy that I had Star, who'd appear at the bottom of my bed most nights, because I felt different from other children. I felt a connection with people who had major problems in their lives, as if I could feel their pain. Soon, Star was to show me what that meant.

On one occasion, I was sleeping and having what I thought was a vivid dream. In this dream, a lady came to me, and I felt a really intense feeling around her. I knew she was a mother, and she was hurt. She had been killed in a car crash. When I woke up the next morning, the emotions of this woman were still with me: she was so sad, and so loving. As soon as I got to school that day I immediately felt I had to go over to a young girl I didn't know. Star was telling me to speak to her. I sensed something was very wrong.

'I've seen your mum,' I said. Star gave me a mental picture then, of the woman from my dream.

'My mum's with the angels,' the child sobbed, just crying and crying. I gently put my hand on her shoulder.

We all have spirit guides, beings in the spiritual realm who protect and guide us throughout our lives. Whether we choose to communicate with them or not, our guide will always be there, helping to make the decisions that empower us and allow us to compassionately help other people. Star is still my spirit guide today. As with friendships, we can have ups and downs with our spirit guides. In my childhood and teenage years, Star was very close at times, while at others I distanced myself from her; I didn't always want to hear what she was telling me and I didn't always want to be different. As my relationship with Star has grown over the years, I've come to accept that she is my constant spiritual companion, guiding and teaching me. When I link with a client, Star is the one who brings through their loved ones in spirit.

I know that Star 'positions me' to be in the right place at the right time so I can have the experiences that I am destined to have in this lifetime. Star is my inner voice, what we'd also call the voice of our intuition. The more we follow our intuition, the more naturally life flows.

In 2006, I was given an amazing opportunity. I wasn't supposed to be at Selfridges that morning; I'd bought an item I needed to change but I didn't feel up to trekking into central London that day. I have suffered from rheumatoid arthritis since my early teens, and some days I'm tired. However, I'd promised I'd meet my friend Claire at Selfridges, so off I went. And I sensed that Star wanted me to be there, too.

While chatting in Dolly's tea room with Claire, I laid out some tarot cards for her. As I was giving her reading I looked up, and was drawn towards a tall, well-dressed man with grey hair walking across the sales floor. *'That's the man who will give me a concession here,'* I said aloud. This gentleman wasn't wearing a staff name badge, and I did not know who he was – but Star was giving me that message.

The gentleman approached our table.

'What are you doing?' he queried in a soft Irish accent, indicating the layout of cards. I explained that I was giving a tarot reading, and that I'm a clairvoyant.

'Can you do that anywhere?' he asked.

We chatted generally for a little while as I explained how I work. He seemed interested, and I felt we connected well.

'I want you in my store.'

'Wow,' I smiled. 'I'm Jayne.'

'Paul Kelly. Managing Director.'

I began Psychic Sisters in a two-room cubicle, and within a few years we'd moved on up to a permanent stand with a crystal shop in a prime location in the store. I have to say, Selfridges have been incredible. They've supported us every step of the way. I'm also blessed to have such an amazing team and a business that's unique; to date, we are the only psychic concession in a department store in the world.

Since that time, the concession has gone from strength to strength. Thanks to Selfridges and the Psychic Sisters team, clairvoyance, palmistry, tarot and angel readings have left the dark backrooms of occult shops and stepped into the bright lights of mainstream society. And what's been great about it is that we often attract people who are opening up spiritually, but don't know where to go. They come across us, and find a whole tribe of women who understand what it means to be intuitive, psychic, a medium or healer – call it what you will – or just 'different'. We often spend time chatting to those who otherwise might not have anyone else to talk to. I'm proud of that. But we took it one step further, too, and began our own 'psychic school', miniclasses for those who are just opening up spiritually. We now teach angel tarot, intuitive writing and aura healing, and offer spiritual counselling.

As Psychic Sisters has continued to thrive, so much has happened for me, too. Talk-show veteran Larry King invited me to read for him on *King's Things*, his show in the US. What a funny, amazing guy he is. I've recently read for the lovely Kim Kardashian, and had the good fortune to film in Los Angeles for other shows over the past four years. But what's been really fantastic is that my work enables me to meet so many people from all walks of life, and I value this so much. We see everyone from celebrities to cleaners, oil magnates to escorts, and Saudi princesses to taxi drivers. We treat everyone equally, and have huge respect for their trust in us. After all, they're often confiding parts of their lives they may not reveal to anyone else.

About the readings in this book

All the readings in the following pages are based on true stories. Some stories have had specific locations, names and other details changed to protect privacy, but the overarching themes and messages are those experienced by me and the other Psychic Sisters (who do use their real names).

Of course, the readings in this book don't always represent my typical day at Psychic Sisters.

Sometimes, I have a week of those truly 'special' readings, when the link with loved ones is strong – and those in spirit want to talk! Occasionally, I can't connect with a client. It may be because I'm not the right person to read for them, or the person in spirit they want to communicate with doesn't want to communicate with me. On other occasions, it can be down to the client. If clients are anxious or desperate, they subconsciously block my link to them.

Here's what happened with a lady from Los Angeles, who had flown in to Heathrow just to see me before returning to the West Coast by private jet (yes, really – these people do exist!). If you're a developing medium yourself, the following account may give you some insight into when you can, and can't, connect – it happens to the best of us.

Talia marched in to my reading room.

'Well, we've flown 3,000 miles just to see you!' she began, dumping her smart Chloé handbag in the corner and settling herself back into a chair. 'I want to see what you can get for me.'

I linked in with Star. Nothing happened. No sensations, emotions, images, movies or inner voice. I tried again, asking Talia to relax a little – she'd rushed from the airport, and perhaps the pressure to be on time was blocking my connection.

Again, nothing.

'I'm really sorry, but I just don't feel it,' I said. 'I can't connect with you. I'll give you your money back now, or you can have a reading with one of the other girls, if you'd prefer.'

'What?' she exclaimed. 'But I don't want anyone else. My husband said your Skype reading for him was brilliant, amazing. I don't see what the problem is.'

'I'm sorry again, but I can't force it if it's not there … why don't you come back in an hour and we'll see if we can connect then?' I was hoping Talia would relax a little in the interim.

As I closed my reading room door, I heard fierce whispering outside. She was talking to her friend whom she'd travelled with. I hoped she wasn't desperately disappointed.

Talia called me when she got back to Los Angeles.

'I was tired, jetlagged and really cranky. I'm sorry, Jayne.'

'Look, when you're ready, Skype me, or come back when you're next in London,' I suggested. 'This time, try to relax, and be more open. You need to have a positive attitude, because if you are demanding, it can block the reading … okay?'

And that's exactly what happened. Three months later, a new, relaxed Talia walked into my reading room, and she finally got the reading she needed.

I hope, too, that you get what you need from this book. If you've downloaded this or picked it up in your bookstore, there's a reason it has come to you today. Perhaps you're curious about the psychic world, you're already involved, or you're drawn to these pages because there's a story here with a message for you. This Psychic Casebook is my way of sharing some very special experiences, and I hope that the words in these pages will touch you, and offer hope, healing and insight – whatever is perfect for you right now.

With love and blessings,
Jayne

www.psychicsisters.co.uk
www.jaynewallace.com

Chapter 1

Annie's Angel

While my heart pounded, pleading, 'Don't turn round! Don't turn round ...' the rational part of my four-year-old brain was saying, 'Annie, why are you so scared? This is silly ... there's no such thing as monsters or ghosts!' I took a deep breath, rolled over in my bed and forced myself to glance down. I froze, terrified of the entity on the floor right next to me. A misty, iridescent figure lay an arm's reach away – and the more I stared, locked in horror, the more defined it became, just like gazing at a strange cloud and seeing it take on a shape. This was the body of a man, huge, broad and glowing white. I could make out two wings tucked under his shoulders. His eyes were closed and his round face was in perfect repose. He was beautiful, like a classical statue, with curly hair – and a face that was unforgettable. I was just a child, and felt enchanted, confused and horrified, all at the same time. I wanted my mum. Then I heard a soft, rhythmic sound: he was breathing, ever so gently ...

Annie didn't want to come for a reading with me at all. Her friend Lyn had dragged her down to

Selfridges and, after her own reading, persuaded Annie to see me. 'But my life is happy, I'm good, so no thanks,' she'd begun, but Lyn was adamant. And within a few minutes Annie was sitting opposite me – all gleaming blonde hair and a great big smile on her elfin face. *'She's decided to go along with it, then,'* I remember thinking. I connected with Annie instantly, telling her about her childhood and the husband she was now with – who had made her incredibly happy. Then, just as we were about to finish the reading, Annie had a question for me.

'Jayne, who was that white man who used to sleep on my floor when I was about four years old?'

I replied, 'Have you noticed that you don't hear the sound of him breathing in his sleep any more?'

'Yes, correct. I haven't, really.'

'That's because that entity is now your daughter. He manifested into her … what's your daughter's name?'

Annie began to cry. 'Her name is Angel.'

Annie says

When I was very small – just four years of age – I woke in the night in terror. I knew there was something on the floor between my bed and my sister's bed. The house was quiet – my parents and my two brothers were sound asleep – but the sense of another presence, so close to me, was deafening. And when I saw him, I panicked. Raised as a Christian, I thought,

This is the Devil! I tried to scream for my parents but I didn't want my sister to wake up and see what I saw … and what if he moved? So I turned back to face the wall, covered my head with the blanket and just wished him away. I prayed, *If I make myself go to sleep now, please, please make him disappear.*

I woke early the next morning and stared at the empty floor. I was expecting to see a white blanket or white towel there, something to explain what I had seen, but it was impossible. There was only clean, brown carpet. But I knew a man was there last night, sleeping next to me … and he was all iridescent white.

I can't say my childhood was a happy one. There was emotional and mental abuse, and I don't remember enjoying being a child or a teenager. Yet whenever I was going through a dark and difficult time, I would hear that calming breathing sound next to me. At first I thought I was imagining it or it was just the breeze. During my teens, when things were probably at their worst, I seemed to hear him more often. It didn't matter when or where I was – daytime, night-time, driving in my car – he always seemed to be with me when I needed some kind of comfort. I became so used to the sound of him that I'd even joke, 'There's my guardian angel again,' and I began to actively like him. I felt peaceful when he was around. He soothed me with his calming breath, and that sound became my friend.

I kept my breathing angel to myself for years, and told no one – until one weekend when, on a whim, I went away to stay with a friend, Sienna. I hadn't seen my flatmate Helen before I left and she didn't know that I'd be away, so when I arrived back home on the Sunday evening I was looking forward to a good catch-up. When I mentioned I'd spent the weekend at Sienna's, Helen blurted, 'No, Annie, you were home this weekend!'

'Helen, I wasn't home. I stayed at Sienna's house last night …'

'No, you were home. I could hear you sleeping in your bed! There was this loud breathing sound coming from your bedroom! You were there – I *heard* you!'

At that point I went cold with goosebumps and my face froze. Helen saw my reaction and I broke down in tears.

'I cannot believe you've just said that!' I sobbed, shocked that after all these years the secret was out. 'That's my angel or spirit guide who sleeps next to me and makes those breathing sounds …' and I imitated the sound for her and she confirmed, 'That's it!'

For Helen to have witnessed it felt like a miracle, a confirmation that my angel really existed. Now my 'invisible friend' was a part of me. I knew he was a good spirit. Funny, he even stayed in my bed when I went out of town. And he even flew to my bedside in hospital when I had open-heart surgery eight years later, making me feel safe as ever with his calming breath.

When, in my thirties, I finally met the man I was to marry, I felt as if the universe had sent another angel to rescue me. My life had been such a struggle, but at last I had found true, genuine love with Michael. I was finally happy, and all I had prayed for and wished for finally came true ... perhaps my angel had listened to me?

Soon we were trying for a baby, and I got pregnant first time. It felt wonderful to extend our love into a family. For some reason, I knew I was having a girl, which was my dream come true.

'Well, if we have a girl, let's name her something positive and beautiful,' Michael mused. The name came instantly into my mind. I said, 'A-ha! How about Angel?'

'That's *it!* Love that name!'

Angel was born on 9 March 2011. The last time I heard my guardian angel's breathing was during the first trimester of pregnancy. Now I can see, feel and touch this beautiful spirit that became my daughter. I love to listen to her sleep, and her breath, the very essence of her life, reminds me of him.

Thank you, my little Angel.

Jayne's Wisdom
This very special story shows that angels are with us right through our lives. Annie's angel protected her through her difficult childhood until she met the man she was destined to be with. After Annie and Michael were married, the angel manifested into their beautiful child, a symbol of their enduring love. Annie's husband is her protector now. I wish them every happiness.

Chapter 2

The Children Who Saw Spirits

Once of my clients, Nita, is a systems analyst. Her husband is a finance manager for a high-street bank. I've read for both individuals, and they are rationalists: they need proof of spirit, which I was able to give them for a close relative who had passed. But one of the other reasons Nita came to me was out of concern for her daughter Sal, seven years old, and her son Ty, nine. The family had just moved countries to a new home.

'Mum, it's so pretty in here,' Sal had told Nita. 'Look at all the colours!'

'What colours?' Nita had asked.

Nita said, 'We were unpacking yet another box in a dark sitting room – we had no curtains at the window. Dusk was drawing in, and I was thinking about putting the lights on. Then Sal said, "Pink, a kind of light blue, green … like a rainbow." Then she began skipping around the room, generally enjoying herself.

'"It's getting dark in here, sweetheart," I said, gently.

'"No, it's not, not with the colours …"'

Nita didn't disagree with her daughter Sal, but instead filed it away for future discussion with her husband. This wasn't the first instance of an odd experience in the house. While the adults had noticed nothing untoward, Nita's son, Ty, was convinced there were more people living there than on the rental agreement they'd just signed.

'There's a man, Mummy,' he'd said, pointing at the long, wide hallway. Nita had looked up, but saw no one there, and nothing reflected in the newly polished parquet floor.

'What does he look like, then?' Nita had decided to play along.

'He's quite small and old, but he looks a bit like Daddy. He's got a long white shirt on like Daddy wears when we go to the temple.'

Nita then told me that her husband confirmed the man was actually his grandfather, whom he'd never met. 'Mikael, my husband, had a photo of him, though, so he went to fetch it. He said, "First, tell me what our son said." So I gave him the description. Then Mikael turned over the photo. And there was a small-boned man, with short, dark hair and my husband's eyes. And he was wearing a long white chemise.'

I linked in to Nita's son. 'He is very spiritual,' I began. 'He doesn't just sense spirits, he sees them in physical form – just as if he's seeing you or me.

'I feel this grandfather is with you in your home to protect you,' I explained. 'There's nothing dark or problematic with your house; it's just that sometimes loved ones visit when you're about to embark on a new phase of your life. And he wants to be around when the new baby comes.'

'How did you know we were trying for a baby?' Nita exclaimed.

'You son has seen her already, and it's a little girl. She's waiting to be born.'

Five months later, Nita came for another reading.

'I'm pregnant, and it's a girl,' she smiled, running her hand over her growing bump.

In cases such as this, I advise parents not to be too concerned about their children's experiences, provided they are not causing them any distress. We all have psychic ability, particularly as children, and often 'grow out of it' – although some of us don't!

When I was six years old, I had a friend called Adele. I didn't realise that no one else in my family could see her. I played with her every week when we went to my gran's house. Adele lived next door, and I'd usually find her playing on the high wall at the bottom of the garden. I'd have to ask her to come down and play with me on the grass, which she did. I'd show her my dolls, we'd make up a game and then my gran would come out with some juice. I never understood why she only brought one cup.

When Gran went back into the house to talk with Mum, I'd offer Adele a sip of juice, but she always said no. She was a tiny little thing, with plaits and a buttoned-up dress like the girls we saw in picture books on the Victorians. I remember thinking she looked a bit strange, but I was just grateful for some-one else to play with. I had lots of brothers and sisters at home so it felt natural for me to be playing with other children all the time. I wasn't used to being on my own.

I told my mum about Adele after a few weeks. Mum was pretty open-minded about spiritual matters – more than I realised. She went to spiritual-ist church regularly, and started taking me with her when I was nine or ten years old. Mum didn't criti-cise or mock me for talking about Adele. She didn't say much, but I felt she kind of accepted it. She didn't push me to 'prove' my invisible friend existed, or give evidence that I had any kind of special talent – unlike my client Georgia.

Georgia had lost her husband three years before we met in my reading room at Selfridges. She'd flown in from Italy for a business meeting the previ-ous day, and decided to pop in for a reading before her flight home that evening.

I brought her husband in spirit through. She needed to know he was okay, and I gave her some messages from him. But I had the feeling she'd heard it all before. So why was she here?

'My son is very intuitive,' she said, after a pause. And then I saw a clear picture of him: a teenager, athletic – and very sensitive spiritually.

'He's been bringing messages through to you from his dad,' I said, as her husband in spirit continued to talk to me through my inner voice.

'Yes,' she confirmed, only half smiling.

'Your husband says, "Stop putting pressure on him."' At this, Georgia looked really irritated with me.

'What do you mean?' she retorted, taking a sip of water, a frown spreading over her brow. 'We get on really well. We're very close.'

'He can't keep doing this for you any more. It's not fair …'

'But he could always link to his father, since he passed away when my son was nine, and I don't understand why he won't do it now.' Her anger was really starting to come out now. *What has she been doing to this child?*

'Georgia, your son linked to your husband easily at first. He's naturally gifted, and the trauma of the sudden death of his father opened up what I'd describe as a strong portal to the spirit realm.

'But now he's a teenager, he's growing out of this: he doesn't want to do it any more. When he's older he might be drawn to spiritual work, if that's his path, but this has to be his choice.'

'It's just … he'd given me messages every week, so I got used to asking him for a message when I was feeling low.'

'And you've become dependent on it.'

Georgia sighed deeply. 'Yes, okay.' She seemed to accept what I was saying, but I sensed she was reluctant to hear it.

'It's time to let go. Your husband doesn't want your son being pressurised.'

The reading room was silent.

I can't say Georgia threw her arms around me at this realisation. Maybe it would take her time to accept that things had to change. She left, quietly, and I didn't see her again. I just hope her boy is happy and following his own path. After all, his father in spirit has his best interests at heart – even when that meant ending the one way he could communicate with his dear wife.

Jayne's Wisdom

Often, psychic ability can be awakened by emotional trauma. Read the life stories of famous mediums, and you'll find that virtually all have suffered in their lives to some degree: serious illness, like me; early bereavement; family break-ups; bullying. I believe that suffering as a child can heighten our intuition and sensitivity, so that we may help others in their lives – but only if and when we are ready to do so.

Chapter 3

The Ten-year Blessing

'There's a man in the room. He looks exactly like you … he's short, with the same complexion. He's with an older woman; he's telling me it's his mother-in-law – your grandmother.'

Elisabetta nodded, blinking back tears.

'I know, he's –'

'Don't tell me anything,' I interrupted. 'I'll talk for now, and you can say yes or no.' I held Elisabetta's wedding and engagement rings as I connected with her father in spirit, and the presence of this warm, protective man filled the room so palpably I could almost touch him.

'He's your dad, and he's showing me the room in hospital where he passed away after a heart attack. No one else was there, just the two of you.'

'But how do you know this?' Elisabetta stuttered.

I kept on relaying the images, the movie playing fast.

'Your dad's saying he wanted it that way, that you'd be the one with him when he passed. You're closest to him. He knew he'd have another heart attack that night, but this time he wouldn't survive. He wanted you to be the last person he saw in this life.'

Shaking, Elisabetta looked right at me, as if to say, *I believe you*.

'He's telling me what you whispered to him just before he passed [this message was highly personal, so I can't repeat it here]. You told him "x" and "x". And he read the note you left for him at his grave after the funeral. The note that says how much you missed him.'

Elisabetta inhaled sharply. 'Yes, *yes*.'

'Don't tell your mum you've been to see me, by the way. Your dad's saying she has never believed in psychics, and she won't become a believer. But you're to give her a kiss, without saying it's from him. And to kiss your son for him, too.'

Elisabetta smiled sadly through her tears.

'Mum doesn't know I'm here.'

I went on, relaying the unbroken sentences flowing from this articulate, warm man.

'He talked to you on your wedding day.'

Elisabetta's eyes widened.

'You doubted yourself for a moment before the ceremony, because the man you married is of a different faith. But he treats you like a princess, just like your dad treated you, and he says that's fine by him. And your dad's saying, "I was with you, guiding you to marry him, because he's right for you. He's a good man."'

I could see the sheer relief on Elisabetta's face.

'And all these years I didn't know if Dad approved,' she sighed. 'And I did question my decision to marry Liam that day, but then it's like a light went on in my head, and I just felt, *this is okay, this is right*.'

'Can I ask a question now?' Elisabetta leaned forward, passing her hand across her wet cheek. 'What about my son?'

'Your dad was with you when your son was born. He's telling me about your labour ... your boy is autistic, and he's not talking yet. Because of this you have an almost telepathic relationship with him.'

'True.' Elisabetta dabbed her eyes with a fresh tissue.

'Your dad's saying that he'll talk when he's five years old – he's four now. And he's brighter than you give him credit for. Start treating him like a little man, because he knows a lot more than you think.'

'That's right, Jason was diagnosed with autism just a few months back. I'm so worried about him not speaking and I'm beginning to think that the autism might stop him speaking at all ... I know he understands so much, even though he can't say it.'

'He'll be fine – he'll talk in his own time.' I could see Elisabetta's little boy running round their house, naming all his toys and asking for his favourite banana sandwiches without a hint of hesitation.

Now Elisabetta's dad's voice began to shift from its gentle, wave-like rhythm to tight, clipped anger.

'Your dad's furious with this business guy,' I continued, 'because he's stolen money from you, from your husband's retail company. It's your accountant. He's calling him a leech, and much worse.'

Elisabetta twisted the damp tissues in her lap.

'When we found out he'd defrauded us, it was too late,' she confessed.

'You'll be okay, Dad's saying. You will recover from this. You won't lose your business.'

'This is just … amazing.'

'Your dad needs to talk again,' I interjected, and this time her dad's words came through me directly.

Dad: 'On my birthday, Lisi, do something for me.'

Elisabetta: 'What can I do? I already visit the grave and leave you flowers …'

Dad: 'Yes, visit the church and my grave, but go just once a year, on my birthday. Afterwards, have a cup of tea and a slice of cake.'

Laughing, Elisabetta brightened. 'Dad, you had such a sweet tooth. And yes, I'll eat cake for you any time you like.'

As the connection with Elisabetta's dad gently faded, I felt drained but happy for her that her dad had so much to say, and so much love and reassurance to give.

Elisabetta says

Dad died ten years ago and, to be honest, I'd struggled ever since. I'm a real 'analyser', and sometimes overthinking got me down. I didn't know if Dad approved of my husband, and I was so unsure about having a reading with Jayne or any other psychic. My whole family doesn't believe in it and I was brought up to dismiss anything of that nature.

That was, until my friend Naomi pushed me into having a reading. I've known Naomi for ever, and she'd seen how hard it had been for me to go through all those big life stages without my dad – my wedding, the birth of his grandson, our life together as a family. She's urged me to have a reading before but I said no; however, when Naomi bought me a gift voucher for a reading with Jayne, I couldn't refuse any longer.

I was very sceptical – I guess as a way of protecting myself. What if Dad didn't come through at all? And what if it was a load of nonsense, and I came out of the reading even more adamant that it was not just rubbish, but somehow morally wrong, too? I couldn't bear the disappointment or anger I might experience.

When I met Jayne, she was so unlike the idea I'd had of a psychic being a weird woman in a dark room crooning over a crystal ball. Jayne's reading room was brightly lit with a crystal chandelier. She was quirky, too – so vibrant and upbeat.

Everything Jayne told me was accurate, including about my time in the hospital with him. She also told me that Dad knew he would pass that night and had engineered it so I'd be there: my uncle was due to sit with him but he asked me to swap with him. Dad had suffered one heart attack and he was very poorly, though he was recovering slowly – or so we had thought. Each member of the family would take turns sitting with him in the one chair by his bed, bringing in food and trying to block out the noise of the hospital, praying for the time he'd be able to come home. The nursing staff gave us no clue that his life was in such danger. So when Dad had another heart attack that evening, it came as a complete shock. He wasn't even 70 years old.

One year on from the reading, my son is now talking – at five years old, just as Jayne predicted. We recovered from that financial blow to our business, too. Dad said we would be okay, and we are. What was also mind-blowing was the detail Jayne gave, particularly regarding his final hours, and also the financial advice that would protect us in the future. Through Jayne, Dad told me exactly how to better manage our business accounts and VAT payments. I had to laugh at this, because Dad worked in legal finance at a major bank in the City before he retired – and he was still advising us from the afterlife!

This reading with Jayne changed my life. I cried torrents – like I'd never cried before, even in those painful weeks after my beloved dad passed away. It was like all the emotions I'd held on to could finally flow out of me. It felt like I could let go of my habitual doubt and uncertainty, too – I used to question myself all the time. Another thing that Jayne picked up on was my OCD; I'd clean the house constantly as a way to deal with my anxiety. I don't do that so much now, because I feel calmer at a deep level – as if everything is as it should be. I don't have to be so anxious, knowing Dad is happy where he is, and that he will always love me.

Thank you, Dad and Jayne.

Jayne's Wisdom

There's always a right time for a reading. Elisabetta's right timing was ten years after her father passed over. So much had happened in her life since then, but she sensed something was missing: his blessing. She needed to know he approved of her marriage, and through the reading she also discovered his unwavering support for her family, and his reassurances about their financial security. To know that Elisabetta had this from her dad gave her peace. I'm just happy I was able to help. I hope, too, that this story might comfort you through any bereavement you have suffered. Our loved ones in spirit are always looking out for us, and their love and healing are there for us to receive whenever we are ready. Grieving is a long, long process, and you can only go at your own pace, whatever that might be.

Chapter 4

Finding William

'Your spirit guide's name is William,' I began, seeing an elderly man in spirit around Laura, my client, 'and he's rubbing his left knee.' Laura had booked a phone reading, but it doesn't matter to me if a client is with me in person or not – I still sense and hear those in spirit around them regardless. And I could see William very clearly: he was showing himself to me wearing a dark suit, which he told me he wore often. Those in spirit often reveal themselves in a favourite outfit, something that the client will recognise. It may be a unique piece of jewellery, a fashion statement, or they may have a treasured object with them; I've had everything from a red ball-gown to a pewter chess set. William's energy, like his favourite whistle and flute, was quiet, reserved. 'He's watching over you,' I confirmed.

Laura didn't know anything much about spirit guides, but she sounded curious – though I sensed she didn't believe my other predictions, including that within the next ten years she would have twins.

'I didn't believe it about the twins, and forgot about it,' Laura later confided. 'And ten years is a hell of a long time. But over the next decade I did think about William often and wondered what he was like. The only thing I knew was that there had been a William, my dad's grandfather on his father's side of the family. I can't explain exactly why I felt such a strong connection with him. Perhaps I simply liked the notion that someone was looking out for me.

'Then, eight and a half years after the first reading, Jayne's other predictions came true, including my having twins. I found myself thinking more about William, too. And I had to investigate.'

Laura called me all those years after that reading to share what she'd discovered. Of course, I had to rack my memory at first to recall the reading, but as soon as she reminded me of William I found this reserved, dark-suited spirit jumping back into my mind once again.

Laura had lots to tell me about her great-grandfather. Born in 1892 in County Derry, William had moved to Belfast as a child. He fought in the Great War and had a daughter, Jean.

'I was so excited, Jayne, when I found out that Jean was still alive,' Laura said. 'I flew to Belfast with my dad to meet Jean and her daughter, Lorraine, to find out more about William. And your description of William was spookily accurate.'

Jean explained to Laura that during his time as a soldier in the Royal Irish Fusiliers William had sustained a knee injury that would trouble him for the rest of his years. Jean also told Laura that the knee was painful, and he often rubbed it. Now I knew why William had showed himself rubbing his left knee; he did it so frequently it had become ingrained as a mannerism.

Laura continued: 'Jean also told me that her father was a quiet man, like you said. His favourite book was the classic novel *All Quiet on the Western Front.*'

I silently thanked William, this quiet man, for being so literal – so that Laura would be able to link the characteristics I'd given her with his daughter's memories of him when he was alive.

'There's just one more thing,' Laura said. 'Remember you mentioned the dark suit? Well, as you know, my dad could barely remember his grand-father (he was only a little boy when William died) and I've never seen a picture of William. After Dad and I had that amazing get-together with Jean and Lorraine, he did some research, and started looking through his mum's photo albums. Yesterday, a letter came in the post from my dad. In it was a photo-graph he'd managed to find of William – the only one that existed. He was wearing his favourite outfit for his weekly trip to the pub. His dark suit.'

Jayne's Wisdom

In spiritual work, you get what you get. If you're given a time-scale for a client, you relay this, just as I did for Lauren, whether or not it fits the client's expectations. Which can go down like a lead balloon (Why can't I meet him *now*, Jayne? I don't think I can wait ten months ...). When I get this reaction, it's clear that the client had an agenda – consciously or not – which they wanted me to validate, regardless of what the universe had in mind.

Spirit guides lead the psychic during a reading. Like William, they also look after us during our lifetimes, just like a guardian angel. (Most angels have never lived on earth, but many spirit guides lived on earth in our lifetime or in previous lifetimes and return to help us.) In the angelic and spiritual realms, time has no meaning. Two years may be the equivalent of two seconds to them, so when we're given a time-scale by our angels or guides it has no weight attached to it. The clients give it meaning – it's acceptable, or too fast or too long to wait, or even disbelief that anything will happen at all.

Jackie, our longest-standing Psychic Sister, shared an example of this with me recently: 'One client, Jasmine, who had just flown in from Lima, was so resistant during a reading that after a few minutes I said, "Look, darlin', you don't have to have a reading with me – go to Nina, or I'll give you a refund." I'd had 15 minutes of her saying, "No, that can't happen

… I can't see that …", and I'm always straight like that.

'"No, keep going," she'd insisted, tight-lipped. So I continued. I told her she'd have a new relationship, and that she'd need to leave her new home – life-changing events that, as a married woman in her dream house, she didn't want to hear. I wanted to say to her, "That's why you're asking me – I'm supposed to be the one who 'sees'." But it wouldn't have helped. Jasmine seemed adamant that the future wouldn't turn out that way as far as she was concerned.

'So, as instructed, I continued the reading. My guide Joseph kept telling me I was right, and I summed up the reading by repeating my predictions. Joseph gave me a "two", which I interpreted as two years; it didn't feel like two months or two weeks. Jasmine shook her head, picked up her Gucci bag and left.'

Two years later, the phone rang at Psychic Sisters' reception. The caller was from Peru. 'Hi, Jayne, it's Jasmine. I just wanted you to know that I had a reading with Jackie Cox two years ago and, to be honest, I thought it was just nonsense. There was no way I could believe anything she predicted for me, but after 18 months each prediction began to come true. Today, I sold my house; now *everything* has come true. Please tell Jackie, because I was really dismissive. But I believe her now.'

Jayne Wallace

Everything happens in what we call 'divine timing'. This is the intelligence of the universe, in that everything happens for a reason at the right time. Our clients might want to see 'proof' of a prediction immediately, but this is just like willing paint to dry or a tomato to ripen. It has to happen in its own time. As psychics, we trust that the timing of the universe will always be perfect.

Chapter 5

Past Lives, Past Loves

'Your dad's saying this, he's saying, "He's not a nice man … keep away from him …" He's talking about your ex-husband.'

'Yes, thank God,' Ivy replied, strangely relaxed. 'I know Dad hated him.' This was one client whom I didn't need to hand the tissues to straight away. I could sense she was sensitive and highly attuned to spirit by the glowing silver light around her crown chakra. She seemed comfortable with herself, this pretty girl, and she had no need to 'look' spiritual – but then few of my medium friends ever do. They're just as likely to have fake tan and lashes as a kaftan.

'Your mum needs you to know that she's healed now she's in spirit,' I continued, seeing another pretty woman, just like Ivy with her neat nose and big sapphire eyes. 'She's showing me she only has one breast. The other was damaged.'

'Mum died of breast cancer when I was three.'

'She's your healing angel, too. I feel that you're a healer.' Ivy told me she'd studied spiritual healing and had travelled outside the UK to help child and adult victims of war.

'My husband at the time didn't understand why I had to go,' she explained. 'It was one of the reasons we broke up. He gave me an ultimatum: stay here with him, or leave and the marriage was over. I chose to go. I had to. And when I finally arrived at the camp, I knew, I just *knew*, I had made the right decision.'

My guide, Star, showed me a huge crossroads and Ivy walking along a golden path, like the yellow brick road from *The Wizard of Oz*. I love that film, and it is one way Star shows me that a client has taken a leap of faith to follow their soul's destiny – the way of light. Star began to show me more about Ivy's future.

'You've met someone new since your husband, a guy who helped you through all the cruelty dealt out by your ex,' I continued, seeing a flash-picture of a smart guy with short-cropped black hair in uniform. 'But I don't feel you can be with him.'

Ivy flinched.

'He ripped my heart out,' she choked. 'I thought, *I've got a chance to be happy*, after all the unhappiness I've been through in my life, and now I don't think he's going to come back …' The tears flowed now. Finding love would have given Ivy hope that she could feel less alone in the world. And now she wasn't able to have love. Why was life so cruel?

'Ivy, this is the reason,' I spoke gently. 'You can't heal his past. He's too damaged from his family, and emotionally cut off because his career demands it. I'm seeing him in uniform.'

'He's a marine,' Ivy confirmed.

'He also has post-traumatic stress disorder.'

'I know,' Ivy cried. 'And I feel so much for him ... but he won't talk. Before, he did, but now he's completely run away and I can't *bear* it. I thought he was my soulmate.' She leant forward, nearly doubled up in pain.

'Just breathe, Ivy, and have a sip of water.' I handed her my Evian bottle. The reading time was almost up, but there was no way I could leave her like this. After our receptionist, Charlie, told my next client I would run late, I returned, reassuring Ivy that she didn't have to leave straight away. Her shoulders softened a little.

'You can't be with him in this lifetime, because it will take him another lifetime to repair,' I explained. 'The reason you have such a strong connection with him is because you were together in previous lifetimes. Part of you recognises this, at a soul level, hence that magnetic need to be together – even if you can't make the relationship work.

'You've also incarnated with your dad in previous lifetimes – he's been your dad before.'

'I know, I know. It sounds crazy, but it's true. It just feels right,' Ivy confirmed. 'It explains so much.'

'And Ivy, you will find real love in this lifetime,' I counselled. Ivy's dad was giving me these words, filling the room with love and warmth.

'I just hope that's true, Jayne.' She smiled sadly.

Ivy did come back to me six months later. She'd managed to separate completely from her marine, and had met a new man, Torr. Relaxed and with such light, bright energy around her, she took a seat and began to tell me about her life since the reading.

'It's weird, Jayne,' she began. 'There's no drama, it's just really easy with him … I don't feel scared or tense that it won't work out. For some reason, I trust him. Like I've known him for ever. Is he from a past life, too?'

'Rather than you having a past life with Torr, this time I feel it's your father in spirit who has brought him to you,' I explained.

'Well, thanks, Dad!' she laughed.

I was so glad that Ivy was happy again – in the here and now.

Ivy says

Having lost my mum at such as young age, I was very close to my dad. I was devastated when he died. Jayne's reading brought me such comfort that Dad was helping me from the other side to turn my life around and finally bring me love again.

Jayne's Wisdom

When you have shared a past life together, there's a sense of being connected at a very deep, purposeful level. If the previous connection is negative, old patterns get repeated until we are able to recognise them and change. If it's a positive, loving past-life connection, we have the opportunity to revisit that love again. Both types of soulmate relationship are very powerful.

Clients come to me who are in, or have experienced, damaging relationships – but they can't seem to leave because there's something so familiar about the pattern they've fallen into. This might be a pattern set up in early childhood (for example, growing up in a home with violence and tension), or it may be due to a past-life resonance we inherited in our ancestral DNA. These beliefs about the soul are now beginning to gain credence. We need to work through these patterns in this lifetime so we can grow as individuals and evolve as souls.

Chapter 6

When Crystals Speak

While most of the Psychic Sisters use oracle and tarot cards for readings, there are some who tune in to their clients by other means – psychometry (holding an object belonging to the client), palmistry, astrology and divining with crystals.

Crystals have a very special place at Psychic Sisters. At the front of our stand we have huge purple amethysts, the crystal of healing, harmony and intuition. Many people love to browse the crystal collection and we always stop to chat with them regardless of whether they're having a reading or not.

Psychic Sister Golnaz – or Naz, as we call her – has a special affinity with crystals and is our 'official' Crystal Reader. She's so sensitive to crystal energy that her crystals are all she needs to see a client's past, present and future. Here's one of Naz's readings to show you how she does it.

My Psychic Casebook

'What are these, then?' Ria asked. 'I've never had a reading like this before …'

Ria was staring at the 12 small polished crystals I'd placed between us on the black velvet tablecloth.

'Choose three,' I began.

'Oh … okay.' Ria began to muse over the multi-coloured stones.

'Just pick those that "speak" to you straight away,' I advised. 'Don't think too much, let your intuition choose for you. Pick up the three you're most drawn to.'

Ria touched a pink rose quartz, then a green aventurine, and finally a pale-purple amethyst.

'Now hold them in your palm, and I mean really hold them. Don't be afraid.'

I'd sensed Ria's fear the minute she stepped into my reading room. She'd started chatting away thirteen to the dozen, and I knew she was nervous. But there was something else, too.

'Thanks. Now hand me the crystals.'

As I touched the rose quartz, aventurine and amethyst, I made an instant connection with her.

'You're being bullied,' I began. 'This situation at work isn't your fault. You're losing your confidence.'

Ria nodded, suddenly silent.

'The first two crystals you've chosen are pink and green, which represent the heart chakra,' I said.

'These crystals attract love and protection, and at the moment you feel unloved, uncared for and vulnerable.

'Amethyst is about protecting yourself from someone or something toxic that's polluting your mind. The name comes from a word meaning "not to be intoxicated", and in legend this crystal was placed in glasses of wine to prevent intoxication,' I explained.

I rolled the three stones together in my palm, and began to see a scenario unfold in my peripheral vision – as if the crystals had opened a door to another room with a movie projector.

'I've had months and months of harassment,' Ria choked. 'Called into the office every week, my emails picked to pieces, questions about my competency …' It was as if the reservoir of pain and rejection was about to burst. I could sense the stress toll on Ria.

'I'm not sleeping, I'm being sick with nerves before work and I'm getting migraines on the way home.'

'The boss who is making your life a misery is incompetent … she's scapegoating you to cover up her own mistakes.' At that, I felt a strong tingle in my palm – the crystals were telling me I was right even before I looked up and saw Ria's sad eyes and her tears.

'What?' Ria blinked. 'But she's said it's my work that's the problem.'

'Do you feel your boss knows how to do her job?'
Ria looked confused.

'How do you mean?' She fidgeted and blew her nose.

'I see your boss was over-promoted and isn't delivering,' I said, 'so she's picking on you – probably because you're nice, you're helpful, and she thinks she can get away with it. She's telling her boss that she has staff problems as a way to distract him from the poor quality of her work. That it's down to you that things are not being done correctly.'

I saw my 'movie' again, and a scene with Ria's boss sitting alone at her desk, way after the others had gone home, struggling with a balance sheet – then going into Ria's email account and reading her emails, looking for ammunition.

'Oh, my God … she seemed friendly at first, but then she began to ignore me, asking other people to meetings and deliberately excluding me.'

My heart went out to Ria. I knew she'd only be in that job a matter of days and that her career as an administrator would soon be over – at least, with this employer.

As if she had read my mind, Ria blurted out, 'She just wants me out, and all I've ever done is try, and keep trying. It's like she's set me a riddle and there's no way I will guess the answer. I get panicky even thinking about it. In fact, I think I've probably had panic attacks.'

'There's no right answer, Ria. She's just manipulated you to believe you're at fault.' I took a deep breath.

'You'll be so much happier in a new job,' I counselled, 'and the longer you stay where you are, the less confidence you'll have.'

Ria came back to me the next week. 'They fired me,' she sighed. 'I'm filing a grievance for bullying and harassment, and they've offered me just one week's wages. I feel so completely drained …'

I gave Ria a black tourmaline crystal, which is one of the best protection stones around. I was concerned that she'd sink into a hole after such a blow, and wanted to support her as much as I could. So I connected with Ria again through the black tourmaline, asked her to let me touch it for a few moments after she had held it.

'Don't dwell on this, Ria – get back out there now. Keep on with the grievance procedure, by all means, but there's a new job waiting for you, and you need to act now,' I advised, as I linked in with her once more through the black tourmaline before returning it to her. I also recommended that Ria try Reiki healing with Catherine, one of our readers and healers, to help release any emotional damage caused by the months of bullying.

Three weeks later, Ria called me. 'I can't quite believe this, but I've a got a new job,' she chirruped. 'I honestly thought I was going to sink into a depression, going over it again and again in my head, in just the way I used to analyse every detail of my so-called "mistakes" when I was in that job. This new role is temporary, but I feel more relaxed there ... like I've escaped to safety.'

Ria says
I keep my black tourmaline in my purse, and it goes everywhere with me. If ever I feel insecure or worried, even for just a minute or two, I touch it. And I'm instantly calmer. I'm relieved I was able to move on from this abusive situation so quickly, thanks to Naz and my tourmaline 'touchstone'.

I (Jayne) know just how people can feel when they're being bullied, and when I come across this in readings I always give clients crystals to help protect them and make them feel stronger. When visiting a south London cosmetic clinic for some treatment, I met Carole, one of the receptionists. She had such a warm, gentle manner and I could tell she really cared about the clients. I also knew I had no choice but to give her a reading, because her dad in spirit had begun to talk to me.

'Your dad in spirit is here, and he's telling me you should be treated like a princess,' I began. 'And that old man of yours, sitting in his armchair at home, just waiting for his tea ... stop running after him. And your boss – Rob –'

'Robin, yes.'

'He's a right bully. He underpays you, overworks you, and you think you should be grateful to him. You've got "mug" written across your forehead. You're worth so much more than this,' I sighed.

'Your dad's saying that if you don't leave Robin he's going to push you right into the ground and make you ill.' Carole looked stunned.

'As one door closes, another one opens,' I said. 'When you do tell him, keep these crystals with you, one in each pocket.' I gave Carole a black tourmaline and a green jasper, which are strong, protective crystals. I knew she wasn't ready to resign just yet, even though she was desperate to. Years of bullying had knocked her confidence so much she didn't believe she deserved to be treated any better.

When I went back to the clinic for my next appointment, Carole was there again. She took me to one side and whispered, 'I still know I've got to leave, but I'm so scared … I don't know if I can do it.'

A month later, I had a strong feeling that Carole would resign from the clinic. I called her and couldn't get to speak to her, but left a message with Helen, the practice manager, who I'd become quite friendly with on all my visits there. 'Please tell Carole, "Do not back down." Thanks, Helen. She'll know what that means.'

Well, it transpired that Carole resigned that morning at the time of my phone call, and she'd got my message straight afterwards. She called me back, and said, 'Jayne, I put the crystals in my pocket, and when I spoke, it's as if the voice didn't come from me. Like I really meant it, like I wouldn't be talked down. I don't know how I said it – it's as if the crystals gave me the right words.'

Carole got another job. An opening for a receptionist came up at Psychic Sisters, and she applied. I'm pleased to say that Carole is now working with us and, as the saying goes, 'As one door closes ...' a new door opened for her – in a place where her kindness and sensitivity are very much appreciated.

Jayne's Wisdom

Crystals are a wonderful way to give readings, like those Naz does, and they are often a source of strength and serenity – the perfect 'takeaway' after a reading is over. A healing session too can help rebalance energy and release past emotions – which is why so many of our Psychic Sisters also offer Reiki and Angelic Reiki healing, either for a short time at the end of a reading or as a separate session.

While crystals and healing can have a very positive impact on our health, we do advise any clients in distress to seek medical advice, or to get further support from a qualified counsellor or therapist.

This is very important for those suffering from anxiety and/or depression, as these conditions may need ongoing advice and treatment from other professionals.

Chapter 7

The Spirit Who Couldn't Wait

'I'm really sorry, Jayne,' my client grimaced as the caller ID flashed up on his iPhone, 'but I have to take this call now.' I made a mock-offended face at him. 'All right then, Mr Important,' I teased – we have that kind of relationship where we can make fun of each other – as he popped out of my reading room and into reception.

I've known this celebrity client for some time. He's a TV presenter, a well-known face on prime-time television, and possibly one of the most spiritual media people I've come across. Our readings together are always relaxed, and I know he trusts and accepts whatever comes through for him.

My door stayed open, and I could hear the voice of our receptionist, Diana, drifting towards me, also on an urgent call.

'It's Debs,' she sighed, not wanting to give me bad news. 'She's got a family crisis – and she's really sorry, but she can't come in to work later.' Debs is a Psychic Sisters medium who works with us once

49

a month, giving palm-readings, so for Debs to cancel meant a pretty big crisis. She's fun and high-energy, always doing more than one thing at a time: 'Cup of tea? Oh yeah, and your love line's broken twice, third time lucky for you, darling. Two sugars?' Clients love her – and she never lets them down.

I asked Diana to arrange cover (*'Phone Catherine!'* was about the gist of it, as Mr Important had finished his call and was making his way back into the reading room).

'All done?' I asked, with a tinge of sarcasm.

He smiled, tucked his phone away, and I turned my attention back to the reading, looking forward to the vibe – some clients are lovely to link in with.

'I'M NEIL!' screamed a voice in my ear.

'Who is Neil?' I blurted.

'I don't know any Neil,' he shrugged.

'I'VE HURT MYSELF.'

'He's telling me he hurt himself. He's saying, "I ran in front of a car."' All I could hear was the voice – no pictures or movie this time, just a poor man in agony battering my ear.

'I know it's nothing to do with me, Jayne,' my client replied, perplexed, and all the banter between us gone. 'You know my friend Adam died from a heart attack, and you brought him through in our last reading – but you're saying this is a Neil, and I've never heard of him, living or dead.'

'I HAD TO DO IT; I WANTED TO GO OUT LIKE THIS.'

'Are you absolutely sure he's not for you?'

'Yes, I'm sure! Who is he?'

'Goodness knows,' I replied, as Neil's bellowing continued, so desperate was he to be heard. I confess, we laughed – it was almost comical, this odd, angry spirit coming to hijack a client's reading.

We continued the reading, but it was hard to concentrate with Neil shouting in my ear every few minutes – and, as you might have guessed, the more desperate he became, the more colourful his language. He used every swear word under the sun to try to keep my attention.

After Mr Important left, I picked up the conversation with Diana regarding Debs's family crisis and, being concerned, decided to phone her at home.

'I'm so sorry, Debs,' I began. 'What happened?'

Debs was in floods of tears. 'My ex-husband died. I just … just can't believe it.'

'When did this happen?'

'About half an hour ago. I got a call from the police. They found him lying on the motorway.'

'Around 10.45 this morning?'

'Yes!'

'He came through during another reading,' I explained. 'And he needs to talk to you.' I could feel Neil's desperate need to communicate with his ex-wife.

'Call me in the morning,' Debs sobbed.

All night long, Neil repeated his message, telling me his name and how he went in front of a car. He was determined to talk to Debs through me – I could sense the intensity building the next morning over my coffee. And I also knew he wouldn't release me until I'd done my job. I'd already called Mr Important earlier that morning to let him know that I'd identified the spirit who'd interrupted his reading, because I wanted to put his mind at rest that Neil certainly wasn't connected with him.

The phone rang in Debs's home in Billericay, Essex. She'd been awake all night, sitting at her kitchen table in a state of shock and disbelief. Her two children had joined her just a few minutes before she picked up my call.

'I'm here,' Debs began. I knew instantly what was going to happen as Neil's voice came through to me even louder than usual. And I had to trust that Debs was ready to hear what he had to say.

'Debs, I'm so sorry, but you know I had to call,' I began gently. 'I've had a man in spirit with me since yesterday afternoon. He's told me his name is Neil, and that he killed himself. He went in front of a car. Now, he's telling me he intended to do this. He walked onto the motorway.'

The line was silent.

Chillingly, Neil began to speak through me. When this happens, I lose a sense of my own voice and channel the voice that wants to communicate. I gave Debs Neil's words exactly as I was given them.

Neil: 'I wanted to do this. You know why. It had to be my way. No one can ever tell me what to do.'

This was anything but a sympathetic spirit.

'All my life it's been nothing but trouble and violence.'

I could sense Debs's vibration down the phone, her fear and grief all at once, her mind flying back to the memories of their relationship like a bird with a bleeding wing.

'You're better off without me. So are the kids.'

Debs: 'Every time we tried you just got worse with the drink and I was scared ...'

Neil: 'I never meant to do what I did.'

Debs: 'You made me scared.'

Neil: 'Then I'm in the best place, aren't I?'

Debs: 'How could you say that? Life with you was a nightmare. But I didn't want you dead.'

Neil: 'I'm where I want to be now.'

Neil then showed me a picture. This was the first time he'd showed me an image – up until now, everything was words.

The picture in my mind was of a building that had been bombed. Small children were crying, trying to climb out of the wreckage. Other children lay life-less. Some of their clothes had been burned off their tiny bodies.

Neil: 'I never could save any of those kids.'

Debs: 'What do you mean?'

Neil: 'You'll know. But I'm truly, truly sorry for what I put you through.'

Neil's voice began to fade as I wiped away tears. I wished there had been more comfort for her, but in Neil's world he believed the comfort for Debs would actually come through his death. This was just the way he thought. And, as a spirit recently passed, he was angry and in shock, too; if Neil ever came to me again, in future months or years, he might be more accepting of his life. Just like us, spirits evolve, on the spirit plane; they may stay the same age, but the fierce emotions associated with their passing can calm.

'My God, Jayne, that was … unbelievable,' she said. 'I'm trembling.'

'You don't have to say anything else, Debs,' I reassured her.

'No, I want to. I have to explain that when I met Neil he was in the military. We were really in love; my perfect man, strong, caring – just everything I'd hoped for.

'But five years into our marriage he was sent to Afghanistan. He did a two-year tour of duty, and when he came home for good he began drinking. I knew he'd been traumatised by something that happened to him out there, but he refused to see a counsellor, a doctor, anything. And he punished me.

I had to take out an injunction against him because he started hitting me and I feared for our two children. He didn't touch them, but they heard the shouting, the screaming …' Debs was crying now.

'He put me through hell. And the worst of it is that, in his heart, he was a good man.'

I gently told Debs what Neil had shown me: the bombed school, how helpless he had felt seeing the children maimed and murdered before his eyes. He had been sent to protect them, but an incendiary device had exploded before they could secure the area. There was nothing he could do. And ever since, he'd blocked out the pain by any means possible.

'Debs, Neil will find peace,' I advised. 'He is in shock now, and he's angry – at the world, at himself. He needs your understanding.'

You might think, 'Why didn't Neil's spirit come directly to Debs herself?' After all, she's a medium too – so why did Neil need me? I felt that Neil wanted an independent messenger who wouldn't soften anything he said, someone without any opinion of him. And, secondly, when we're in shock, as Debs was, it can be hard for even the most experienced medium to connect with a spirit; we naturally protect ourselves and can subconsciously block the link. However, in this case, Neil made it abundantly clear that I was to be his communicator, and that I'd say his words just as he wanted.

As we ended the call and I returned to my now cold cup of coffee, I felt relieved that my work for Neil was done; I sent a silent blessing to this wounded soldier who needed, above all, to be forgiven.

While this is an extreme instance of spirit 'interruption', there are many examples of gentle nudges we psychics get when a spirit is ready to talk – usually at the end of another reading. It's like they're queuing up to speak, and when it's time they'll make their presence known.

Psychic Sister Sheila, who is also our concession manager, gave me this intriguing account of one of her readings.

Psychic Sister Sheila says
'It's Mr Dennis for you, Sheila,' our receptionist, Coco, said as she ushered in a tall, anxious man – anxious from the way he leapt into the reading chair and handed me a necklace without missing a beat. Which, as soon as I touched it, released such a loving, female energy that I knew that this lady in spirit wanted to communicate.

'Okay, I'm ready,' I began, silently asking my guides, 'Can you give me something to help him?'

My whole body erupted in pain. *I hope this helps him*, I screamed in silent agony, *because it's not helping me!* I tried to relax and accept the agonising sensation in my stomach – I never fight the feeling a spirit gives me, because they're doing it so I can give their loved one evidence that they're in the room. I just hoped it would pass – and soon. I exhaled, and thankfully the words began to come.

'I'm feeling such pain in my stomach ... this was such a cruel illness.'

He nodded, his eyes filling.

'She died from aggressive stomach cancer.'

I then told him, 'I love you, darling.'

'And I love her so much, too,' he replied. 'She was so brave.'

'She's okay,' I reassured. 'She's happy and she's with her cat – a little white, sweet kitten with begging eyes.'

He smiled then, a really huge smile, as a tear crept down the side of his nose.

'She didn't have the best musical ability!' I grimaced, hearing a strange screeching sound.

'She was a terrible violinist, but she loved music. When she played, the kitten ran hell for leather out into the yard.'

For the first time he smiled, and it reached his eyes.

Just as I was about to finish the reading, I felt something else.

'Ooooh, that's strange ...' and suddenly I pictured a slow-motion scene of a jeep coming towards me, then a deafening bang.

I must have paled, because he asked, 'Are you okay?'

I nodded, then Coco knocked on the door to tell me it was 3 p.m. and time for my next reading – which was odd, as 3 p.m. is my scheduled tea break.

I focused back on Mr Dennis to see him looking at me strangely.

'I don't understand,' he said. 'She wasn't involved in a car accident!'

'Don't worry, it's obviously not for you,' I concluded as I went to shake his hand. 'Bye, Mr Dennis ...'

'It's Jonathan,' he said. 'My name is Jonathan.' Obviously unfazed by my random comment about a car crash, he surprised me with a huge bear hug, and I tried not to cry, too – I'm a big softy at heart.

I opened the door, expecting my next client.

'No, not till 3.30,' said Coco. 'I just wanted to keep you on time for your break.'

At 3.30 on the dot Olivia, a well-dressed woman in her fifties, sat down and told me straight: 'I want to see if my daughter is okay.'

I began to shuffle my tarot cards, and again felt that huge bang like a firework, and saw the same vehicle hurtling towards me – a repeat of exactly what I'd seen at the end of Jonathan's reading.

'Is your daughter in spirit?' I ventured. 'I keep seeing this car ...'

'That's it,' she confirmed. 'Alice was turning out of a junction on her bicycle and a car came out of nowhere. She was thrown right up in the air.'

At once I felt that Alice had been here a while, waiting to see her mum – from 3 p.m., when I'd finished my previous reading with Jonathan on time.

'Olivia, is there any chance you were going to be here at 3 p.m. today?' I hoped I was on the right track, otherwise I was going to look pretty stupid. And I didn't want to cause this lady any confusion and compound her sadness. Alice had only passed away three months before, and her grief was raw.

'It's so weird,' she replied immediately. 'I'd made an appointment for 3.30 p.m., but was thinking I wasn't going to come after all. I'd ummed and ahed all afternoon. Then I looked at the clock. It said five to three – if I was going to keep the 3.30 appointment I'd have to decide now if I was going to go through with it or not. At 3 p.m. I made the decision to come.'

'Alice came through to me at exactly 3 p.m.!'

'Oh, my word,' Olivia laughed. 'You know, Alice was the most punctual girl. She would even be ready for school ten minutes before her brother and sister, waiting on the step with her sports gear all perfectly packed ...'

As soon as Alice's mother committed to attending her reading, she'd made sure she was there. It was the right time for Olivia to connect with her – the first time since her passing – and the right time for Alice to talk. She is a very loving spirit, and she said some special words that gave Olivia comfort. When loved ones in spirit communicate with those they leave behind – through words, pictures and feelings – we know that love goes on. The bond between them is never broken.

Chapter 8

The Trauma Readings

Before you commit to this chapter, be aware that the following readings are tragic and sad, and involve violence. I can't pretend all my readings are sweetness and light – they are not. If you're very sensitive, you might prefer to skip this chapter altogether, which is absolutely fine. I have to include it because this type of story does represent the kind of client I often see, and the readings that come with it. As you might expect, they don't have happy endings, but these clients often get information about a loved one through my reading that helps answer long-standing questions – and allows them to begin to heal, and make peace with the past.

The Boy from Hamburg

'Do you want some water?' I had to ask the elderly gentleman opposite. My reading room was boiling hot. The air-con was on the blink again, and I was peeled down to a vest top. I had been guzzling

Evian all afternoon, and this was my last client of the day.

'No, not for me,' he replied. He placed his cane on the floor and settled his hands in his lap, sitting straight-backed in his chair.

Josef looked as though he had stepped right out of a royal palace. Impeccably dressed in a tailored suit and waistcoat, he sat calmly opposite me in my reading room, worrying at one of his cufflinks – no doubt emblazoned with the family crest, I remember thinking. I knew nothing whatsoever about him other than that our receptionist, Sheila, had told me Josef had flown in from Paris that afternoon for his appointed reading with me. Many of my clients are international, so there was nothing particularly special about this. I glanced at him as we introduced ourselves, and I noted that his face was what you'd call distinguished – but it's never the face I look at when I'm in the flow of a reading that involves spirit contact. What I see more clearly are those on the other side that my clients bring with them, which to me can be even more vivid that the client in the flesh.

'Well, okay. We'll begin with a tarot reading and I'll also ask you for an object of yours to hold to help me link in to spirit,' I explained. I always begin my readings this way. But this one was going to be different: before I could ask to hold his watch, or one of those cufflinks, he looked directly at me with flat grey eyes. And I felt the most intense emotions

running through my body – every part. I have rheumatoid arthritis, which some days is very painful.
But when I make such a deep and instant link with a
client it's as if my illness steps back to let me do my
job – and the emotions come flooding in.

It was time to start talking, which is what I always
do as soon as I have a link. And I have no choice but
to continue once the first words are out.

'I have your sister; she is standing right behind
you, touching your hair. She killed herself; she is
with your dad and five brothers. They have all passed
over and are together now.'

Josef continued his impenetrable gaze and his
expression was neutral. 'I came here to find out
about my finances,' he said, enunciating each word
slowly. 'So you do not lay out the cards for me, no?'

Usually I link with a client through cards and by
holding an object, but Josef's sister in spirit was
already here; the temperature in the room plum-
meted and the cards stayed mute in their pile on my
reading table. This traumatised spirit was not about
to be stopped in her tracks.

The link intensified. I could feel more extreme
sensations in my body and her presence filled my
small room. I have angels, Buddhas, huge amethyst
geode crystals and every type of beautiful spiritual
object on display, but when someone in spirit wants
to come in this strongly it's as if my little room
doesn't exist. And neither does Selfridges: just

outside our Psychic Sisters concession in the store is a mad frenzy of shoppers, music, beautiful books and all manner of distraction. But Josef, his sister and I were about to enter another realm altogether.

I consciously opened up more to this sister's energy, allowing her words and pictures to come through. When I make spirit contact it's like a movie is running in my head, playing out events from their lives on the earth plane from start to finish. And Josef's sister had much to share.

There were very graphic images of her with a rope around her neck, showing me how in desperation she had taken her own life.

'Why?' I silently asked her.

'I could not go back to Germany,' she whispered. 'It's where my father and brothers were murdered.'

I gave Josef her exact words.

Then Josef's father stepped forward. The energy changed instantly and I felt an intense pressure at the side of my head. This man's body was rigid with fear and I felt that a gun was being held to his temple – I could almost feel cold steel. But he was about to tell me exactly what was going on in this cold, cruel place.

'Nazi!' the father shouted, pointing to a German soldier. Like a movie, I saw another soldier with a gun turn and point it towards the father's two sons. The boys were shot in front of him, and I was shown Josef's father bent forward, devastated by shock and grief. The two Nazi officials then proceeded to shoot and kill Josef's father. I felt the first shot in my body, a pain so agonising I felt as if my left ribcage would shatter. *Was this how Joseph's father died?*

I breathed through the pain. Josef had uncontrollable tears streaming down his face and I suddenly felt the overwhelming sadness of Josef and his father in spirit, the grief of father and son in two different worlds connected through me. And now I couldn't control my own tears, even if I had tried.

I had to go on with the reading: Josef's father was still pulsing his emotions through my heart and I knew there was more that needed to be said. I took a breath and gently asked him, 'You witnessed this, didn't you?' He glanced upwards with a look of defeat.

'Yes.' He reached across the table and held my hand, sobbing quietly. I could feel him trembling.

Josef's father came close again, this time to show me more detail. It's common that those in spirit who passed in a traumatic way need to show me exactly how they passed when I connect with them.

The movie began to play again. Josef's father showed me a bullet passing through his left lung and out behind his shoulder blade. A little boy, Josef, was running to his father and crying. He was trying to get the bullet out of the wall behind, where it had become embedded in the brick. That was just the first bullet. There had been more.

For a moment, I stepped out of being Jayne the psychic because I had a question. I asked softly, 'I am really confused. I thought that the Nazis gassed the Jewish people and others held in concentration camps; were they shot, too?' He returned my gaze.

'My father and brothers were shot, not gassed. My mother died from starvation.'

We sat in silence. The clock on my wall ticked on.

Josef's sister stepped back in, with the energy of his father fading. And she had one more piece of evidence for her brother.

'Please tell him to get my emerald and diamond ring out of the wardrobe where he keeps it now,' she whispered. She told me her name: Rosa.

'That was the ring of our grandmother, and has been passed down the family for many generations,' Josef sighed. 'Our mother did not live to wear it, so it was to go to my sister, Rosa.'

'She wants you to hold it when you need to feel close to the family. She knows how much you miss them all; she knows the anger you feel even now. While you cannot forgive, you can accept.'

Joseph paled. 'She knows about the depression, the anger …?'

'She has such a loving energy around her.'

Josef smiled.

'She's telling me, "Don't sell it. The investment you made is safe now, and you won't lose everything again."'

After our goodbyes, I knew that within a minute or two Josef would be back on Oxford Street, and then home to Paris. I shared a cup of herbal tea with the girls, and drank a silent toast to one amazing survivor.

Josef says

I was born in Hamburg, Germany, in 1934. In 1943 we were forced to enter the Neuengamme concentration camp in Bergedorf, near Hamburg. There were six of us children, and my mother and father. Only Rosa and I survived. After liberation in 1945 we were taken to relatives in Saint-Omer, northern France. Rosa was 14 years old when our father and brothers were murdered. I was six, and Jayne was right: they shot my father in front of me. I will never forget this and I still cannot forgive, all these years on.

Rosa wanted to return home to Hamburg after university, but she had a nervous breakdown. She hanged herself with a rope during her first year as a student at the Sorbonne in Paris. If the support had been there for victims then I think she would have been saved somehow. But this was 1950. I was 14 at the time I lost my sister, the same age she'd been when our father was murdered.

What Jayne did was extraordinary. I came out of the reading not only shocked that Jayne knew so much about my family, but I felt a little less alone. My family in spirit hasn't forgotten me.

Jayne Wallace

A Son's Last Wish

'I don't know why I'm getting this, but I'm seeing a camel,' I began.

'Camera?'

The refined gentleman sitting opposite had misunderstood me; English was Mr Ahmed's second language, and I guessed he was tired, having just flown in from Kuwait that morning. He'd perched himself on the velvet chair, and opened with the enigmatic line: 'This is going to be a very important meeting.' He'd also brought a sealed bag with him, which he placed down by his feet very tenderly. I didn't think too much of this at first; many clients come laden with luggage and shopping.

'No, it's definitely a camel.'

I'd linked in with Mr Ahmed very quickly, bringing through his mother in spirit. But now we'd switched to the camel; it felt like the most ominous creature I'd ever seen, totally unlike those benign, soft animals we see on holidays.

Mr Ahmed bent forward, holding his stomach as if in pain. Either the camel was hugely significant to him, and he was in shock, or he was in great despair; he'd travelled 3,000 miles to London for a reading and the first specific symbol I'd got for him was a camel – almost a cliché, given his origins in the desert country of Kuwait.

Was I way off beam? I pushed the thought away. Over the years, I've learned to trust my guide, Star, implicitly, and I tell my clients exactly what she shows me. And Star was just getting started.

Suddenly, I saw the camel again, this time as in a movie; it hurtled across a desert road and into the path of a car driving at breakneck speed. Inside the car, Star showed me three young men, their jaws dropping in horror at the split-second realisation that the animal was directly in their path.

'The car came off the road, crashing in seconds,' I relayed. 'The young man at the wheel wearing a blue T-shirt was your son,' I said softly. 'There was nothing they could do.'

'He was driving too fast.'

'Yes, on an open road in the desert.'

Mr Ahmed was crying softly, and he opened the bag he had placed near me on the floor.

'This is the T-shirt my son was wearing when he died,' he explained.

I held the item in both hands and began to connect more deeply with his son, 24-year-old Kafir.

'He knows he was driving too fast, but he didn't anticipate any danger, and the three of them were having fun. He is telling me he was happy until that moment, and he felt very little pain; he passed quickly.'

Mr Ahmed nodded.

'But he's also saying it took days before you found him.'

'The authorities found them, and took them to a hospital morgue. They didn't contact me; I was searching for my son for three days. I thought he had become lost on the desert roads. I was desperate to find him, and then the phone call finally came. I felt like my life had ended, too.'

'Your sister's telling me that you should marry the woman you're with now,' I interjected. Those in spirit have ways of interrupting the flow sometimes, but it's always with an important message.

'She says this woman will make you happy, and help you with some of the pain of losing Kafir.'

'I wanted to marry her before he died,' Mr Ahmed confessed, 'but I've felt so low that I've almost switched off from her. I don't know if she can wait for me.'

'She'll wait.'

Now Kafir wanted to talk again, and I sensed that aunty and son were together in spirit. Mr Ahmed's sister had passed over ten years previously, and she had brought through Kafir, who had passed just two months ago, to help heal some of her husband's pain.

Now it was Kafir's turn. And I liked this strong, upbeat man.

'Your son wants you to be strong for him,' I continued. 'He was always such a positive, sociable person. He is telling me he came to London to study, which is why you've come here – not just for a reading, but because you feel part of him is here, too.'

Mr Ahmed shifted in his seat and looked at me directly, nodding.

'I know we are Muslim, but Kafir liked the occasional drink. He loved the London lifestyle. He's telling me that you two had a drink together in a bar here.'

'Yes, I should be a good Muslim and never drink, but you're right – I shared a beer with my son on that occasion.'

'The bar's near here, on Greek Street. He's saying, "Dad, meet me there for a drink, one last time."'

With that, Mr Ahmed picked up his belongings, left my reading room and went to have a beer with his precious son. I like to think of this brave man sitting at the bar, knowing his beloved son was right next to him, forever smiling.

The next day, I had two more readings that were unusually dramatic – even for me. While I know I attract many clients who have suffered a great deal of trauma in their lives, these next two readings are almost beyond belief (although, aside from name changes and some specific circumstance changes to protect confidentiality, like all stories in this book, they are true).

I believe that, as psychics, we attract the clients we can most help. We often see themes in readings that reflect our personal life experience and abilities. As a writer, Liz gets queues of clients with writer's block; Jackie, who is very direct, like me, attracts clients whose loved ones in spirit may need to tell them off! Sheila is highly sensitive, and many of her clients have suffered bullying and abuse.

Maybe because I'm an experienced medium, I see many people with violence in their past history, and sense how to relay messages in a way that empowers them. It's one thing to be able to tell someone what's already happened in his or her life, but the purpose of a reading is to be able to make sense of the past so we can move forward. Unfortunately, there's a perception that when receiving a reading it's best not to say anything or 'give anything away'. While I understand that some clients wish to do this, when I've told them the story of their own lives, there needs to be something else: a new understanding, a reason for what happened in terms of that person's soul journey, or a way to heal. This happens in conversation after what I call the 'download' part of the reading. It's like saying to someone, 'This is what you need to know; this is what happened in the past. Now what do you want to do with that information?' We get spirit contact for a reason: because they want to help us from the other side. It's not about a medium saying, 'Look at how clever or accurate I am about the past.' Why tell a client what they know about themselves already? We have to do more than that – to be able to answer questions, to show possible alternative paths that the client may choose to take. While validation is important – providing evidence of life after death – psychics and mediums are not fairground attractions. We take what we do very seriously. And we want to help.

Raj Finds the Truth About His Father

Raj was a guy I really wanted to help. He sat far away from me in my room, which is unusual, as it's an intimate space (translation: small). He actually looked ill, sweating and fidgeting like he wanted to bolt.

'There's something I need to know, and no one else so far has been able to help,' he began, speaking slowly. English was his third language, he later told me, but he was word-perfect.

No pressure there, then, I thought. I actually felt I might block any connection, which can happen when a client is desperate, but my guide, Star, had other ideas, and she linked me with a man in his late thirties who looked very much like Raj: medium build, jet-black short hair – his father. This man was wearing a dark suit and white shirt that was stained and crumpled. And then the movie began to play.

'There's a man in a car, he's telling me he's your father,' I began, describing him physically. 'He says there was "foul play". He's with three men in this car and they are holding him somehow. He can't get out. They're driving in – like – an urban area; now it looks industrial, factories, deserted roads, no houses.

'He can't speak in the car because they won't let him. It's hot and dry; he's dirty. The man in the passenger seat has a gun.'

I was shown the vehicle moving fast and erratically over scrubland, hurtling further away from the town, dust rising from the tyre tracks. It was the dead of night outside and I connected with the terror that Raj's father was experiencing. Star kept the movie rolling and I had a bad feeling where this was going.

'They've stopped the car. The taller man in the back is dragging your father out, the man in the front passenger seat is moving round to the back of the car, taking your father's other arm; he's resisting but they are forcing him down on to the ground.' I didn't want to go on with this, but Raj's father was going to show me what happened. Or so I thought.

Instead, I felt the most excruciating pain on the side of my head. My head jerked violently backwards and my knees hurt. I knew Raj's father had been forced to his knees on the dirt road.

'I'm so sorry, but your father was shot,' I said gently. 'He didn't survive.'

Raj bowed his head.

'I was a child when my father disappeared,' he said, wiping away another tear. 'No one would tell me why, only that he was never found, and presumed dead. He was with me, in our house with my mother, hut was called to a meeting late at night. He worked as a diplomat, so late calls were not unusual at the time. But he never returned. Now I know why.' Raj heaved a huge sigh.

'You're the first person to tell me how he died.'

'He was fighting for a cause that was unpopular, politically, and he had enemies.'

'Yes.'

'You were young when it happened. Right after your eighth birthday.' Raj's father was showing me a cake with eight candles.

'That was the last time I saw him.'

The throbbing in my skull was beginning to ease.

'Your father was a brave man. He's proud of you, too, and he sees you going far in your career, but he's glad you're not in politics in your country. It's still too dangerous.'

'I know he's around me,' Raj nodded. 'Every birthday since he went away.'

'I'm so sorry about what happened to your father,' I consoled.

'I'm not sorry that you told me. I always sensed there was some bad reason for his disappearance. I'm just sorry I've had to wait 20 years for the truth.'

With that, Raj leaned in towards me, squeezed my hand, and left.

Jayne Wallace

Muna's Lost Childhood

'I was so, so scared, and it went on for years. Years.' Muna looked up at me through wet lashes. 'As soon as I was just nine, it began. He came in to my room and touched me at first, saying it was just a game, but not to tell Mum. It got worse, and he raped me on my tenth birthday. I believed him when he said he would punish me if I ever told, as if what he was doing to me wasn't bad enough.'

As soon as Muna strode into my reading room for her first appointment, a colour flashed over the area of her womb. This petite woman in a tailored suit and Hermès scarf appeared composed – tough, even – but I linked in with her before we even spoke, through the sad orange swirl I sensed below her stomach. There was no sunshine in this colour; just orange dulled with wide smudges of grey.

The tainted orange told me instantly that Muna had suffered greatly in her past, and her fertility was being blocked. Just as I was beginning to focus more intently on this strange colour, my guide, Star, began to show me a movie of Muna's abuse: a father creeping into his little child's room while her mother was asleep. Sickened, I blocked out the image as quickly as I could.

'I know you want children, Muna, and that the sexual abuse you suffered as a child has damaged you so much emotionally that it's blocking your ability to conceive naturally. The fear is locked within you –

the fear that your husband will do to your children what your father did to you.'

She nodded, a tear running down her cheek. 'But I was so, *so* scared …' All her tightness began to dissolve, as I realised her tough exterior hid such great vulnerability.

I felt a new link, then – an older man connected with Muna's husband.

'I've a gentleman with me. I feel he's related to your husband – his grandfather.' I described him; he showed himself holding up a pair of boxing gloves.

Muna paled.

'He passed away five months ago. And yes, my husband told me he'd been a fighter in his younger days …'

'You'll be a wonderful mother,' I interrupted, because this feisty man wanted his message to get through now, 'and you'll never put your children through the sheer torture of your own childhood. Your husband is a good man. You know that.

'He's also telling me that your husband has to be a dad, it's his life path.'

'I know … I feel so useless. We've been trying for children for four years now. And we've failed so far because of me; I'm the reason.'

'I can see two children for you, through IVF.'

'I was thinking of having it, but –'

'You're scared. Don't be. This grandfather is helping you. He's looking out for you both.'

Well, I'm happy to say that two years later Muna brought not one baby in to say hello, but two – perfect twins. I smiled down at her two beautiful boys who gave me identical, chubby grins.

Muna says
Thank you so much, Jayne. I feel you gave me the confidence to have treatment, and, through the message from my husband's grandfather, the confidence that history wouldn't repeat. IVF was hard, but it has brought me the two most beautiful gifts.

We called my first-born twin Azi, after my husband, and our second boy we called Sami, after their great-grandfather, who came through in my reading to help me. God bless him.

Jayne's Wisdom
When clients have gone through horrific sexual, physical and emotional abuse, my first impulse is to cry with them, and sometimes I do. But I have to do my job: to bring through messages that may just offer some comfort and hope for the future.

I've seen many clients over the years with incredibly sad histories. Josef, from the first story, said he came to me to ask about his financial future, but his sister and father desperately needed to acknowledge him, and to do this they had to replay the most painful memories of his life. I never want to cause a client distress, but those in spirit deal only in truth, and they come through to tell the greatest truth of all: that love goes on after their passing. Mr Ahmed, Raj and Muna's loved ones in spirit came through me to offer hope, support and never-ending love.

After readings that involve trauma and bereavement, I do advise clients to consider counselling if they need it. Also, after bereavement, I don't recommend that clients visit me for at least another six months, when they will be further on in their healing process. It's very tempting to want spirit contact with loved ones regularly, especially when the passing was recent and the client is still in shock.

Some clients can become dependent on psychics as a way to heal their pain. A first reading can give them the reassurance that their loved ones are safe and at peace, but to continually ask for contact with a person and spirit often feeds the grief. Only the bereaved person can fully heal themselves. At Psychic Sisters, we've had to ask several clients not to return after discovering that they had seen two or more of us over the course of a few weeks. We always try to help these people as best we can, while gently explaining that we can't see them again so soon.

Chapter 9

True Love … and a Liar

These two stories come from women who didn't intend to have a reading, but something – or some-*one* – guided them to me. While this type of reading might begin with, 'I came to see you because I was curious,' or, 'My friend saw you and recommended you to me …', there's always a deeper reason: our guides and loved ones in spirit need us to see the truth to keep us on our life path. See what you think.

Anjhula's husband

'Tanaya recommended you,' Anjhula began, pushing her sheen of long black hair behind her ear. 'So I thought I'd come, too, for a reading.'

I was captivated. We have some extraordinary clients at Psychic Sisters, but the instant Anjhula sat in my reading chair, with her tanned, never-ending legs and face that could launch a thousand lipsticks, I knew, too, that there was more to her than met the eye. As soon as I connected with her I sensed she had serious intelligence as well as looks, from the books my spirit guide, Star, was showing me floating around her shoulders. And the pink glow from her heart chakra told me she was about to meet, or had met, 'the one'.

'I can see you study, there's textbooks around you … you're analytical, academic.'

'Correct.' I could see this lady wanted proof I could do my job; her beautiful face was impassive. (*The sort of expression I would only achieve after a session of Botox*, I mused.)

'You're highly qualified.' I was about to mention her work as a model, but I sensed she'd think I was 'cold reading', basing this information solely on her obvious model looks.

'Correct. I've just finished my master's degree.'

I paused for a second as I felt it was time to lay out some cards for her. As I did so, I felt a strong connection with an older man in spirit: a protective, traditional man who loved her.

'I have your grandfather with me, and he has some messages for your father.'

'Yes, he passed away three weeks ago.'

I relayed the messages (I don't repeat them here, as they were personal to Anjhula's father). She seemed to accept them, and promised to give them to her father that evening.

'How many siblings do you have?' I asked, seeing brothers and sisters around her.

'You tell me.' I knew she had two siblings but I'd asked a question instead of just giving the answer. Even though I'd just channelled her grandfather, Anjhula still wanted evidence that I was genuine.

'Two.'

'Correct.'

I went on, as my spirit guide, Star, was beginning to get into full flow now.

'The guy you're dating, he'll be studying business in New York – in two years' time, and you'll go with him. You'll be living there. If you want to marry him, you will.'

'No way,' Anjhula protested, this time letting some emotion through. 'London's my favourite city. And I'm not even dating.'

'You'll be seeing your future husband very soon,' I concluded. I could say no more than that.

Two years later, Anjhula came back.

'I saw my husband at a dinner I went to soon after our first reading,' she smiled. 'I'd met him once before, but this time I paid close attention to him … and he did ask me to marry him! And he got a place at business school in New York, where I'm now studying for a PhD in International Psychology at Columbia University. But I don't know where we'll end up next.'

A few days later, Anjhula's husband booked a Skype reading with me. I told him that Malaysia would be a good move for him, and that I saw oil.

Anjhula called me after the reading.

'How did you know we were thinking of moving to Kuala Lumpur? My husband is considering taking over a palm oil company. You know he's pretty sceptical, as I was, and he can't believe your prediction.'

As I always say, the proof is in the future.

Anjhula says

I met Jayne Wallace on the recommendation of a friend. I had just finished my master's degree at University College, London, and thought it would be a fun treat – little did I know how much her readings would come to support and guide me.

Being the psychologist that I am, I gave a different name when booking the appointment. I was sceptical, and I wanted it to be impossible for Google to 'help' the reading.

When Jayne told me I'd move to New York, she just looked at me as if to say, 'You're thinking from the secular level; I connect in another realm.' She described my future husband to a T: eye colour, religion, height, his family, tastes and attributes, yet with a specificity that cannot be down to chance or luck.

As a trauma psychologist in the media, I am trained in the scientific/empirical way of thinking; on the other hand, I experience every day the fickle nature of the entertainment industry, in which everything is transient and sometimes inexplicable.

My experiences professionally and personally around the world have taught me humility, and not only to acknowledge the existence of another realm, but to embrace it. Turning to a psychic or even a psychologist as a crutch might foster co-dependency, yet Jayne emphasises empowerment. She's not there to give you directions, but to serve as a mirror, to provide solace and encouragement in a way that no amount of technical or scientific knowledge could.

Yvette's husband

'He's a lying, cheating rat!'

As this forthright spirit spoke to me, I thought, *We've got off to a right old start*. My client, Yvette, hadn't even taken off her coat.

I felt a really strong, motherly energy from this woman and I knew this was Yvette's mother in spirit. When I connect with a loved one in spirit, the first thing they do is show me how they passed as evidence for the client. But Yvette's mum wanted to get these words out first. Then she showed me, through my body, how she had passed, so I could feel how she felt. This is what's called 'clairsentience', when the spirit gives us the sensations they experienced when they passed away. It's also one of the most immediate ways for a medium like me to understand a medical condition, and I sensed Yvette's mum didn't have much time. Instantly, I felt as if all the air was being sucked out of me.

'Your mum passed away due to a lung condition,' I began.

Yvette sat down.

'I'm connecting strongly with your mum … and she's not too happy about the way your husband is at the moment.' I'd decided, for once, not to repeat her first statement word for word – at least until I knew Yvette could deal with it.

'Why not?' she grimaced. 'He's a *really* lovely guy.'

'He's not, your mum says.'

'No, you're completely wrong. He's a really good man.'

'But I've got to say what your mum is telling you. I've got to say that he's having an affair.'

'Never.' Yvette crossed her arms in defence, not wanting to hear a word more against her husband.

'Okay, fine. I understand you don't want to hear this, but I think you should listen to your mum.' As if to help me persuade Lisa that her mum was right, she told me more, and very quickly in case Yvette decided to march out of the reading room in disgust. I had to get this out now.

'You tell her,' her mum said, 'go home and look in the top shelf of the kitchen cupboard. He's got £4,000 in cash stashed away in a shoe box.'

'We've got no money like that in the house!' Yvette protested.

'This is your proof. Go and see if the money's there. When you find it, your mum says you need to keep it.'

Yvette was listening now.

'On Thursday evening, follow him. He'll go to a house. Park well away from the house so he doesn't see you.'

'Well, I don't think you're right,' she huffed.

'Promise me you'll do this … your mum is showing him sitting down, having dinner with his other woman.' I could see this bold, strong mother right next to Yvette.

'My goodness, her legs are even longer than yours!' Yvette laughed at this – I didn't say it in a derogatory way, of course, but I could see Yvette's mum next to her and couldn't help comparing their bodies!

Back to business, Yvette's mum commanded.

'She's saying, "Yvette, don't argue with me!" Call me early next week and let me know what happened,' I finished, as Yvette got back into her coat in a fog of disbelief.

The reading had lasted just 15 minutes.

Low and behold, I got a phone call from Yvette. Like her mum, she didn't hold back.

'He's a liar!' she spat.

'So … you followed him, then?'

'Yeah. I saw him park then go into this house, only a couple of miles from where we live. I waited for about ten minutes, then knocked on the door. An older woman answered the door.

'"Is Gary there?" I shouted. Well, Gary just strolled up through the hall to the front door, all stone-faced, and I was so angry I slapped him and ran past him into the house. Some family was sitting at the dining table, all laid out nicely for a roast. And then this younger woman who was sat with them says, "Who's *this?*"

'So I screamed, "I'm his wife!" I was so angry, Jayne.'

'Was your mum right, or was your mum right?' I said.

'He was supposed to be at a meeting after work.'

'And you've kept the money, like your mum asked?'

'Yes. The £4,000 in the box, and he's not getting it back. I'm having the money, and his girlfriend is welcome to him.'

Yvette says

My mum passed away nine years ago and I'd never had any contact with her until I met Jayne. And god knows why I went to see her – I was a bit sceptical, but my sister had seen Jayne and enjoyed her reading. With hindsight, maybe my mum was guiding me to her. I hate coming into London on public transport – I'd do anything to avoid it – but still I found myself battling my way on a train and two tubes to get there. Something I'd just never do willingly. I can see now that my mum wanted me to go to Jayne. She'd kept silent all those years but decided she had to step in to protect me from further deception. And in the months after the reading, I got to know just what an unpleasant man I'd married, when all the time I thought I had the perfect life.

After I discovered his affair, we broke up and he moved out. Then our youngest daughter needed a blood transfusion after an operation, so the doctors asked her father if he would be a donor for her – he and our daughter have a rare blood group. *He refused.* While I was shocked at his affair, this was the lowest of the low – to abandon our desperately ill daughter and not appear to care if she survived. Thankfully, the hospital staff, who were brilliant, managed to locate an alternative donor in the north of England. I'm so, so grateful to that young man in Sheffield, because he saved my daughter's life.

After the split, my daughter, son and I were left with nothing – apart from the £4,000 that I found in the kitchen that Mum told me to keep. I used that to pay the rent for a few months until I could get some benefit support sorted – my part-time wages don't pay enough to keep us all. Needless to say, Gary gave no money for the children and has cut off all contact with them. I'm so thankful I saw Jayne and that she got Mum's message through about the £4,000. Without that, we would have lost our home.

Thanks, Mum, for what you did.

Jayne's Wisdom

In Yvette's case, her mother had guided her to me – as if she'd decided 'enough was enough'; this lady gave me specific information that would get Yvette out of a relationship founded on lies. For Anjhula, her grandfather guided her to me because he didn't want her to miss out on getting together with her future husband. And because Anjhula had had a reading, she told me she paid her husband-to-be 'particular attention', and began to feel a strong bond with him. Without this awareness, would she have been so open to meeting a partner?

So, if you feel like having a reading and don't know why, it could be that one of your guides or loved ones in spirit is taking you by the hand and leading you towards someone who can give you the messages you need. Even when it's a message you think you don't want, your guides will always find a way to tell you the truth.

Chapter 10

Where Earth Angels Tread

Jackie Cox is one of our longest-standing psychics. She's a real character, and certainly doesn't hold back when there's an important message for a client. Jackie's spirit guide, Joseph, connects with loved ones in spirit, and gives her their messages (and if she doesn't hear him right, he'll shout in her ear until she's word-perfect!).

In this amazing story, Jackie's warning for Bev was so critical that her father in spirit 'recruited' some Earth Angels to repeat the warning. Their shocking revelations, which came months after Jackie's original reading, made even my hair stand on end. Here's Bev's story, in her own words.

Bev says
'I've a message from your dad,' Jackie began. 'He's saying to me, "You don't want to be the richest person in the graveyard."' Well, I smiled straight away at that – this was one of my dad's favourite sayings. I'd had psychic readings before, gone to

spiritualist church and even one of those audiences with Sally Morgan, hoping to get a message from him, but nothing had ever come through. And now, 30 seconds after sitting down in Jackie's reading room, she said she had my dad with her. *Was this for real?*

Jackie looked for no reaction from me, and set about her work, her bracelets jingling as the tarot cards flew from her manicured fingers to the reading table.

'You're working way, way too hard,' Jackie continued. 'I can see this has become the norm for you – you work morning, noon and bloody night, darlin'. And you're looking after your son, too.'

I said nothing, and just nodded. She was so spot on I felt myself filling up.

'He's got amazing eyes – big, like yours, and he's very special. Artistic.'

Archie, our nine-year-old, loved everything to do with art, and I encouraged him lots. I work as a designer and illustrator, and every now and again we went art crazy, covering half the house with our pictures. We were a right couple of Jackson Pollocks when we had the chance, throwing paint onto huge pieces of paper and generally enjoying ourselves.

'You can't do everything, Bev,' Jackie continued sternly, interrupting my reverie. 'Your son is happy, and he's doing really well at school. I can see you're very close to him, and there's a special bond. But you have to look after yourself properly. If you don't, I can see the stress affecting your health.'

I knew Jackie was right, but to be honest I've always worked hard. Call it my northern work ethic, but as a freelance designer I can't always choose the projects I take on or know what's involved until I'm committed. Basically, it meant that every night after Archie went to bed at 8.30 p.m. I'd get back on the computer and work until 1 or 2 a.m., sometimes through till 5 a.m. if I was on a deadline, then get up again at 7 to get Archie ready for school. And for the last three months I'd worked every weekend – doing all the daytime stuff he wanted to do, like taking him swimming and to karate, then working like crazy to do more work before I had to pick him up. My husband helped, but he runs a building business and isn't home as much as me. Basically, I had no free time. And for some reason, I just couldn't walk away from my current project because I didn't want to let anyone down.

'You're exhausted, and your dad's telling me, "Stop now."'

Jackie was right. My dad was a man of few words but when he did say something he meant it. Thing is, I love what I do, and that's my problem. It's not as if I hated my job and couldn't wait for the weekend. I'd just somehow decided I'd fit everything in, like most mums, I suppose.

Jackie told me more about my relationship and family, and the reading went by in a flash.

'Remember what I told you,' Jackie concluded, and gave me a hug. I felt a bit tearful when I left, and decided I'd cut down my hours – when the current project was done. *Just another eight months of hell*, I thought.

Time ticked on. I kept up the gruelling hours, hanging on to the fact that it would all be over soon. But it wasn't. The deadline got extended for another three months and the client was piling on more work daily. I had to design eight children's books, and project manage them as well as commissioning the illustrations. The deadline was horrendous, so I worked day after day. I started feeling bad physically – headaches that wouldn't go away, lack of sleep, no energy – like I had a virus or something. I started getting palpitations and my chest would feel tight, but I ignored it. I'd sort everything out as soon as I handed in the work.

Then something odd happened. After dropping Archie off at school one morning, I bumped into one of the other mums. I'd seen her a few times doing the school run – she had two children in the year below Archie – and she looked so tired and sad. We'd nodded to each other now and again, but never spoken. Then she looked at me, sighed, and said, 'It's not been a great time for me. My sister died on 24 November of a heart attack. She was only 51.' Before

I could reach out to her and talk, she turned back to her car and drove away. I felt shocked and sad for her, but at the same time I wondered, *Why did she tell me that?* I hardly knew her. And what was even stranger was that 24 November is my birthday, and I was also 51.

I climbed back in the car and realised I was shaking.

Was this a message?

Four days later, the phone rang.

'Hi Bev, it's Simon.'

'Simon?'

'Yeah, I know we've not spoken for ages, but I kept thinking about you. Yesterday, I walked past HarperCollins Publishers on my way to the hospital … I've had a stroke. I can't believe it, but I must have been really, really stressed out. I'm having rehabilitation at Charing Cross Hospital and for some reason you came to mind …'

To cut a long story short, Simon talked for half an hour about his condition. I hadn't heard from him for 15 years – he had my mobile number still, and I haven't changed it in all that time. We'd worked together at HarperCollins in Hammersmith way back, and saw lots of each other then, but we hadn't had contact since. But here he was, out of the blue, on the phone. Simon was a few years younger than me, and had always looked fit and well. He was a real personality, too, and a great guy to work with.

'Take care, Si. Really hope you feel better soon ...'

'I'm still in shock. I'm just hoping I'll be able to work again.'

We finished the call. My heart went out to him. *How strange*, I thought. Calling me, out of everyone he knew.

Back home, I popped the kettle on and switched on my computer. Another 12 emails demanding decisions and asking me to do more than I'd agreed to, yet again. And there were more emails from the organisers at the community centre chasing me to give them extra help with a display for the children's art show. So I got going straight away and vowed to get through all the queries by lunchtime. I'd had three hours sleep that night and wasn't feeling too bright. By 1 p.m. my chest felt tight, like I couldn't breathe. My heart was racing. I stood up. It was as if a fist were clenching my heart and my arms had started to ache so badly. Feeling dizzy, I knew I was beginning to panic. I phoned my sister, Cath, who lives round the corner. 'God, Cath. I feel like death. Can you come round?'

An hour later, I was sent to Barnet hospital, still in pain with palpitations – like I had no control over my body any more. I actually thought I was having a heart attack.

In triage, my phone rang. I saw one of the art show organiser's names flash up on the phone, but

Cath grabbed it and answered. 'Jan, there's no way Bev can do anything else to help,' she said, exasperated. 'She's exhausted with everything she's been doing, and she's now in hospital.'

Two days later I was sitting at home listening to the recording of Jackie's reading for me. The warning was there when I'd had the reading – 11 months ago. And dad, of course, had been right. Thankfully, I didn't have a heart attack, but it was a serious panic attack that had put me in hospital. And after that I stopped working. It scared me so much I'll never work like that again. I was killing myself – for what?

I can see now that, through Jackie, Dad got the message to me, but I didn't stop work. So he gave me the message again through the mum at school, and again through Simon, like he knew I was in danger and he was doing everything he could from the other side to protect me.

I'm listening now, Dad. I know you won't have to tell me again.

Jayne's Wisdom

Earth Angels are often ordinary people who act as messengers. Our angels and spirit guides choose people we will see day-to-day when they need to communicate with us urgently. You'll recognise an Earth Angel because this person will say something unexpected or out of character. Often, these people are not close friends; they are acquaintances, neighbours, the woman you meet in the park while you're walking your dog, even the postman. Earth Angels can be the most direct way to get a message through. Angels can send us signs that we're on our life path – feathers, pennies, recurrent numbers – but at critical times in our life we need to hear the message loud and clear, in words, not symbols we have to decode. From this we can learn how important it is to listen to everyone we encounter, because they just might be Earth Angels in disguise.

Acknowledgements

This book would not have been possible without Liz Dean – author and Psychic Sister, who has shared my vision and brought my words to life – and the amazing team at Psychic Sisters – Golnaz Alibagi, Jackie Cox, Carole Holliday and Sheila Young. The wonderful Charlotte Tilsbury, Diana Madison and Belinda Carlisle have also played such important roles in the unfolding of the Psychic Sisters story. I thank you all. My fiancé Lee Ryan deserves a very special thanks for his unwavering love, guidance and support over the many years we've shared.

My agent Chelsey Fox is one of those special people who understands what I do – thank you, Chelsey. And thank you to the following contributors who have shared their experiences: Ria, Anjhula Mya Bais, Laura Milne, and Bev Speight and her son, Archie. I also send gratitude to the contributors whose stories appear here, but are not named in this book. Thank you – you know who you are.